On Their Own

Adventure Athletes in Solo Sports

By Steve Boga

BOOK ONE

HNB

International Standard Book Number: 0-87879-925-7

10 09 08 07 06 05 04 03 02 01
5 4 3 2 1 0 9 8 7 6

Library of Congress Cataloging-in-Publication Data

Boga, Steve. 1947–
    On their own: adventure athletes in solo sports/by Steve Boga.
      p. cm.
    Summary: Describes the training, determination, and personal
triumphs of such athletes as motorcycle racer Kenny Roberts,
long distance runner Ann Trason, and speed skater Eric Heiden.
    ISBN 0-87879-928-1
    1. Athletes–United States–Biography. 2. Determination
(Personality trait) [1. Athletes.] I. Title.
GV697.A1B555   1992
796'.092'2–dc20
[B]   92-15762
                                                         CIP
                                                          AC

Contents

Kenny Roberts

Kenny Roberts in Top Form

Kenny Roberts
King of the Road

Kenny Roberts sits on his motorcycle at the starting line. He is wearing a red and white leather suit and a white helmet. He is not the biggest racer. He may even be the smallest. But he is the best. Yet it wasn't always so. Kenny will always remember one of his first races just as if it were happening today. There were thirty other bikers in that race. Everyone was opening and closing their throttles, revving their engines. The roar was so loud, Kenny couldn't talk to the guy next to him.

At last they were off! Thirty riders on thirty motorbikes were trying for the lead. The air was filled with the spray of sand. And the noise was loud, like a swarm of giant bees.

Kenny was first off the starting line. He was leading the race at the halfway mark. Then his front tire hit a hole. He spun out of control. Then another bike hit him on the side. He flew from his bike like a shot. He hit the track, then rolled and bounced. Ramming into a wall head first, he went limp.

As he lay there, dazed, dozens of bikes skid and slid within inches of his head. Dirt filled the air. Suddenly, another rider rammed into Kenny's bike. The twisted metal flew over Kenny's body.

After that, Kenny learned how to stay on his bike.

Some say Kenny started racing when he was born. Even then he had a quick start. He was born two weeks early. His parents blamed it on a hit-and-run driver who smashed into the family car before Kenny was born. Some say Kenny has been getting back at bad drivers ever since.

As a boy, Kenny was small and loved horses. Most people thought he would become a jockey. He says, "I was a cowboy. I liked horses, not motorbikes."

When he was 12, a friend got a mini-bike for a present. At first Kenny did not want to try it. But his friend kept pushing him. So Kenny rode the bike, but only for a minute. He says, "The first thing I did was drive it into a house trailer. It scared me to death. It also thrilled me."

It thrilled him so much that he tried again. After that he decided he wanted to be a good rider. So he practiced all the time. "Two months later, I built my own mini-bike out of a bicycle frame and a lawn mower engine," he says.

At age 14, Kenny began racing the dirt tracks of central California. Even as a young rookie, he was very cocky and very good. By the time he was 16, he was known in all the small valley towns. He was beating everyone his own age. They even made Kenny start behind the other racers just to make it fair. Still he won. People either loved or hated him. But they came to watch him race.

The rules did not allow him to turn pro until he was 18. But he did not care. He says, "Motorbikes were just fun to me. It wasn't a job. I was working in a repair shop and riding the canals with my friends. I was having fun. The faster I went, the more fun it was. And since I was good, people put faster bikes in front of me. They would say, 'Ride this!' It was fun to show them I could."

At first no pro team wanted him. They thought he was too small to race motorbikes. The big bikes weighed about 300 pounds. Kenny then weighed 110 pounds. But he had a great feel for motorbikes. When Yamaha did sign him to a pro contract, he turned out to be the best rookie in the country.

Kenny says, "Being big doesn't help." (He should know. He is now 5 feet, 5 inches tall and weighs 135 pounds.) "Good riders are not big guys. To race, you need good reflexes and quick muscles, like a boxer. But you also need to dare to go 45 minutes full out. You can't ever relax. Racing is hardest on legs, wrists, and forearms."

As a biker, Kenny sits a lot. But he still has to be in great shape. Weeks before a race, Kenny starts working out. He runs, plays racquetball, hits a punching bag. Sometimes he lifts weights. But most of the time he rides motorbikes. He rides a mini-bike for reflexes and a motorcross bike to build muscles.

By the time he was 26, Kenny was the best cycle racer in America. He was married and making more than $300,000 a year. He was happy. But Yamaha, his sponsor, wanted him to race in Europe. That was the big time. That was where he could make real money. So he took his wife and kids and went to Europe. He was off to be a Grand Prix motorbike racer.

At first, the European racers did not pay any attention to little Kenny Roberts. Why should they? He did not look like much. And this was the Big Time. Speeds were more than 180 miles per hour. And it took years to learn the courses. Nobody went to Europe and started winning right away.

Nobody, that is, except Kenny. He won three of his first five races. Then he went on to win the whole thing. He was the Grand Prix World Champion.

He was the first American and the first rookie ever to become champion. After that, the other racers noticed him. In fact, they tried not to let him out of their sight. And they gave him a nickname. They called him "King Kenny."

For the next six seasons, Kenny really was the king. He was the best road racer in the world. And he was exciting to watch. On turns, he would lean his bike so far over that his knee would drag on the road. Before Kenny, no one else dragged his knee. Soon everyone was doing it.

Kenny says, "It is a game of inches. Lean an inch too far and the bike scrapes the ground. They then scrape me off the pavement. An inch the other way and I lose the race."

Sometimes an inch can cost more than a race. It happened when Kenny was testing a new Yamaha bike in Japan. He was all alone on the track. Maybe that was the problem. Maybe without other riders he relaxed.

He came into a right turn. He hit the front brake and his bike slowed to 120 miles per hour. He had done it a million times before. But this time was different. He suddenly lost control of the bike. It slid out from under him. He was thrown hard against a guard rail and knocked out.

He hurt his spleen, broke his foot and his back. He nearly died. But Japanese doctors saved him. They put him in a cast and sent him home three weeks later. They told him, "You will never race again."

Three weeks later, when he went to the hospital for X-rays, the doctors were surprised. His back was healed.

"Good," Kenny said. "I'm racing in Austria in a few days."

"Impossible," the doctors said.

"Watch me!" said King Kenny.

So six weeks after he almost died, Kenny showed up in Salzburg, Austria. People thought he was there to watch. When he pulled his leather suit on over his back brace, they knew he was there to race.

He raced and he won! The other riders could only shake their heads in awe.

The next week, he finished second. Then he won three straight races in Italy, Spain, and

Yugoslavia. He went on to win his second straight World Championship. He did it wearing a back brace.

How did he do it? How did he come back? Lots of people would have just quit. But Kenny had no quit in him. "Breaking my back was just a hurdle that I had to get over. It was something to make me better," he says.

He could not have been too much better. In all, he won the World Championship three times. He became a star. In Japan and Europe, he was treated like a king. They sold thousands of posters of King Kenny leaning his bike into a turn.

He says, "People do not know me in America. I am not famous in the United States like I am in other countries. I can walk down the streets of my home town. Most folks do not even know me."

Kenny has always been serious about motorbikes. He has made millions of dollars being serious about them. But he is also a man who loves his fun. He loves to joke and laugh. A child at heart, he once broke his leg goofing around on a motorbike with his kids. "The most fun you can have on a bike is just riding around with your buddies or your kids," he says.

Kenny has won races by going faster than other riders. He says though that the real thrill of riding is not high speeds. It is learning how to do it right. "I enjoy taking a 20-mile per hour curve at 30 with perfect brake, gear, and line. It's better than going 170 miles per hour on a straight road," he says.

Most people sitting on a 150-horsepower bike would die of fear before it ever reached 170 miles per hour. Yet Kenny, who has hit 190 and had a blowout at 170, says he has never been afraid on a bike.

He says, "I have felt excitement, but not fear. During a race there's no time to be afraid. I have been nervous before a big race and worried about doing well. But that's not fear. And after a near miss, I have thought, 'Hey, I could be dead.' But then it's not fear anymore, is it?"

For a little man, Roberts is very strong in the arms and legs. But he thinks he has won most of his races because he has a strong mind. Kenny says, "The mind has to focus. Sometimes I get near my limit, and I know I could die. But I still think hard about doing it right. You see, this is what I do. I race bikes. It is an exciting sport because I have to get it just right. A good guess does not make it."

Yes, Kenny is tough both in body and mind. He says, "I can be nasty. I have always been very pushy. As a kid, I was mean and stubborn."

For proof, Kenny points to his very first race. He says, "I was riding a nasty old bike, a 50-cc clunker. It died on me not far into the race. I got off and kicked it."

That was the last time Kenny got off his bike before the finish line.

Lynne Cox on Dry Land for a Change

Lynne Cox
Solo Swimmer

Lynne Cox swims in cold water better than anyone alive. She fell in love with water when she was eight years old. Her family was living in New Hampshire. Her grandparents lived on a lake. It was important that Lynne and her brother and sisters learn to swim. Then they could safely enjoy the lake.

Her older brother entered races. He joined a swim team and won some medals. Lynne decided she would like that, too. She joined the same swim team. And then her two younger sisters joined the team.

One day the kids told their dad that they wanted to be great swimmers. Their father liked that idea. He never pushed them. But if they wanted to try to be good, he was ready to help.

He decided to move the family to Southern California. There were more places to swim and a longer swimming season. And the coaches were better.

Lynne joined a California swim team. There she met Olympic coach Don Gambril. He saw at once that she was a special swimmer. She had large bones, huge shoulders, and great energy. She could swim for hours and never get tired. She was 5 feet, 6 inches tall and weighed 180 pounds. Some would call her fat. Her coach would just call her "great."

He also saw that she did not belong in a swimming pool. Lynne agreed. She loved swimming, but she was tired of going back and forth between the walls of a pool. She needed to swim free. She needed to swim in the ocean where she could go on and on.

When she was 14, Lynne entered three ocean swims. They were one mile, two miles, and three miles in length. She won all three! Lynne loved being out in the vast Pacific Ocean. "Everything opened up. It was like going from a cage to freedom," she says.

When she was 15, she broke a world record by swimming the English Channel in 9 hours and 57 minutes. It was the fastest time ever for a man or a woman.

Then one day her father pulled out a map and changed Lynne's life. He pointed to the tiny body of water between Siberia and Alaska. "What about swimming this?" he asked.

She thought about it. "The Bering Strait? There is no way I can do that. There are probably icebergs. Nobody could swim that."

The map was put away, but the idea would not leave. Lynne began thinking, "Well, maybe it could be done."

For the next 11 years she swam in cold

water all over the world. She did swims no one had ever done before. But she could not stop thinking about the Bering Sea. "I wonder—could it be done?" she thought.

Finally she decided to swim it!

She would swim 2.4 miles from one island to another. One island was near Alaska. The other island was near Siberia. That meant she would be swimming from the United States to the Soviet Union. The Russian people of the Soviet Union and the American people had not always been friends.

At that time the Soviet Union was a closed country. People there could not always do what they wanted. Visitors were not welcomed. Lynne had to write the government of the Soviet Union. She asked if she could finish her swim there. First the Russians said yes. Then they changed their minds and said no. Lynne kept writing letters.

She says, "I wanted to do the Bering swim

because nobody had ever done it before. But I also thought it might bring the two countries closer together. I thought in some small way I might help the world."

Lynne did not hear from the Russians. She decided to make plans anyway. She set a date for the swim. She then worked hard to find sponsors and a crew. She would need help from lots of people to do the swim.

As the Bering swim neared, Lynne trained six days a week. She swam three hours a day in the Pacific Ocean. She also lifted weights to make her shoulders strong. When she left for Alaska, she was feeling fit and healthy. Of course, the water near Alaska would not be like the water near Los Angeles. It would be much, much colder.

Lynne and her crew were just about to leave for Alaska when word came. Good news! The Soviet Union had agreed to send a boat to meet her halfway through the swim.

When Lynne got to Alaska, a thick fog hung low over the Bering Sea. The water was gray and choppy. It looked scary. It also looked cold. It was in fact 38 degrees. That is only slightly warmer than a snow cone. But Lynne was not going to use the grease that many ocean swimmers put all over their bodies. They think it keeps them warm. Lynne does not think so.

She says, "There are four big problems with grease. One, it doesn't work. It warms you less than one degree. Two, if you get in trouble, your crew can't pull you out of the water because you're too slippery. Three, it smells so bad, it makes you sick. Four, it is made from animal fats, so it draws fish. Some of them have teeth. And out there I do not want to attract the wrong kind of crowd."

Lynne will not use a wet suit either. She says it helps a swimmer float. "I try to swim under my own power. And a wet suit is

22

cheating. It is like taking an elevator to the top of Mt. Everest," she says.

Lynne hoped that she would be able to slide into the icy water. But there was no beach. She would have to dive in from the rubber boat. The sudden chill would be a real shock to her body.

The whole village of 150 people came out to wave goodbye to Lynne. She climbed in the rubber boat and waved back. Some of the children blew up balloons and let them go. They made bright colors against the gray sky and sea.

Lynne took off her heavy coat. Now she was wearing only a thin one-piece bathing suit. She pulled her goggles over her eyes and thought, "Gee, this is a dumb thing to do." Then she jumped in the water.

"Aaaahhh!" The cold was like a thousand knives going through her body. But she could not think about that! There was a long way to go. She would think about good things. Her mind was so strong, she could do that. Even when her body wanted to give up, her mind was able to take over. She thought, "Feel the water flow over your body. Now feel your body flow through the water."

An hour later, Lynne was still going. She was swimming at a steady 72 strokes per minute. She knew she was getting close to halfway. That was where the Russians from the Soviet Union were going to meet them. They would then guide her to the finish. But it was so foggy that she worried they would not be able to find her.

Lynne looked strong and steady to the writers and doctors in the boats behind her. She looked like a swimming machine. But she did not feel like a machine. She hurt like a human being. Her feet were numb and her shoulder ached. "Where was halfway? How would she know when she got to Siberia?

Would there be a place to buy a Coke?" she wondered.

Her mind stayed as busy as her body. She thought, "I have to keep going as fast as I can. The longer I am in the water, the more dangerous it is. The longer I stay wet, the more pain I feel. Boy, is it cold. No, don't think about that! But my feet are going numb. Don't think about them either! I wish the boats would stay in front of me. They are supposed to guide me. I am not supposed to guide them! Relax now. Stay steady, stay strong, and relax."

The doctors in the boat wanted to check her body heat. She rolled over on her back. The doctors held a wire tied to a stick over her belly. It sent a signal back to the boat. It told the doctors how cold she was.

"Lynne, you have only lost one-half a degree of body heat," a doctor said. He was smiling. If she had been too cold, they would have pulled her from the water.

Lynne smiled, too. Then she went back to swimming. It was nice to know she was not going to die, not yet anyway.

She saw the boat through the fog. There they were! "The Russians are coming," she thought. It was a 30-foot Navy boat. She could see the men looking over the side. She wondered, "Why are they not smiling? Did we do something wrong? Maybe they changed their mind again. Maybe . . . "

After two hours in the icy water, Lynne was beat. Well, she was almost beat. She was hanging on. But she thought about quitting for the first time.

She was fighting a cold ocean current that tried to push her north. She was afraid she was too tired to win. For a second she thought, "Maybe I will let it take me. Maybe I will let the water take me all the way to the North Pole. No, I will run into solid ice long before I reach the North Pole."

Then she saw it! She saw the island. She was almost there! With a new burst, she found her stroke. She swam at 66 strokes per minute. She did not feel tired anymore.

Lynne completed the most amazing swim ever. She was in icy water for 2 hours and 9 minutes. She finished on Big Diomede Island. The Russians welcomed her like an old friend. She brought good will to a place that almost never sees Americans.

A writer in one of the boats called it "The most dramatic single sports feat I have ever seen."

She swam in water in which few, if any, people in the world could swim. How was she able to do it if no one else could? What does she have that other swimmers do not have? Here are four likely answers:

1. Lynne was born with genes that gave her the skill to swim well. As a kid on vacation

in Maine, she could stay in cold water longer than anyone else.

2. She has the right body type. Fat makes up 18 to 25 percent of most women's body weight. But Lynne has almost 35 percent body fat. That helps her float and holds in her body heat.

3. Over the years she has trained her body to stand cold water. This is called conditioning.

4. Desire. This is hard to describe, but Lynne has plenty. She has the drive and the desire to be the best.

Lynne is still doing long, cold swims. She has given up a lot to do what she wants. For one thing, she does not make much money. Sometimes she gives talks about her swims. But any money she gets for speaking goes right back into another swim project.

At age 33, she still lives with her parents so that she does not have to pay rent. The love of her life is swimming.

Has it been worth it? Lynne says yes. "Swimming is my way to health. It's how I can reach out to the world. One of the best moments of my life was when I finished the Bering Strait swim. I reached up and felt the warm grip of the Russian man's hand. It told me, 'You made it.' Not just me but all of us had made it. It came down to that link between the two hands."

Dave Scott—Triathlon Events

Dave Scott
Ironman

Dave Scott was getting ready for the Hawaiian Ironman. He stood in the warm ocean up to his knees. He shook out his shoulder muscles. He wanted to be loose before the 2.4-mile swim.

He looked around at the other triathletes. There were more than 1,000 men and women. The men wore yellow bathing caps. The women wore red bathing caps.

He wondered, "How did they do it? What drove them on?" He thought that most of them would be happy just to finish the race. As for him, he tried to win.

A triathlon is three sports in one. After the

swim, comes a 112-mile bike ride, then a 26-mile run.

No wonder most people just tried to finish. The people back in the pack would take more than 13 hours. Dave would take less than eight hours. He was one of the very best in the world.

It was 7:00 a.m. and the air was warm. An hour later when Dave came out of the water, it would be hot. He liked that. His body did well in hot weather. "My sweat glands do a good job," he says. That is why he had won the Ironman four of the last six years.

The big clock ticked toward zero. Some people began to count: "Five . . . four . . . three . . . two . . . one . . . " A cannon boomed to start the race. A thousand swimmers began slapping the water. In the middle of the pack, the water was white and choppy. At the front where Dave swam almost alone, the water was still blue. Dave slipped into third place, doing

84 strokes a minute. He was content there.

He was second out of the water. Dripping wet, he ran to the bike area. He rinsed off with fresh water. He put on socks and biking shoes. He ate a banana and put some figs in his pocket. Then he climbed on his bike and pedaled out into the warm sunshine. In all, it took him less than two minutes from ocean to bike. Now he was in first place.

The bike phase would be 112 miles long. It would take Dave more than 5 hours. That gave him a lot of time to think. He pedaled and thought. He thought about how he got started doing triathlons . . .

Dave had been a good athlete in high school. But he was not great. His best sport was swimming. In college he played water polo. He became an All American in that sport. But after college, he didn't know what sport to try.

Then in 1978 a bunch of Navy guys invented the Ironman Triathlon. They combined a swim, a bike ride, and a run into one event. Then they raced to see who was the best. To do that sport, you had to be an ironman. That was how the race got its name.

The next year the Ironman was on TV. At home in Davis, California, Dave Scott watched that TV program. He thought, "Hmmm, put three sports in one. That sounds like a good idea. I bet I could do that."

He bought a bike. He began training in all three sports. No one had ever really trained for a triathlon before. Every day Dave would swim for two hours. He would then run for two hours. Finally, he would bike for three or four hours. His daily workout took about eight hours. He says, "I thought if I trained more than anyone else, I had to win. If I found out that someone else was training 50 hours a week, I would train 51."

His practice paid off. In the 1980 Ironman he led from the start to the end of the race. He finished in about eight hours. He beat the next best guy by more than an hour! He beat the record by two hours!

He says, "It is amazing. I am not the best in the world in any of the three sports. But put them together and I can be the best."

Why can he be the best? What does he have besides big muscles? Well, he also has a strong mind. He says, "I was a physical education major in college. I learned about the human body. I learned what muscles do. I learned what foods to eat. I think knowing that has helped me a lot."

Dave has also learned how much to eat. The answer is "lots." At 6 feet and 163 pounds, he is not fat. But the way he eats, you would think he would be. It is said that he has eaten 17 bananas in a day. Another time, he ate five salads for dinner. He has to eat that much because he works so hard at his job. He is a triathlete.

_____

Four hours into the Ironman, Scott, calves bulging, stood up on the pedals of his bike. He was riding up a hill into a hot head wind. All around him were rocks and brown earth. This sure was not the pretty part of Hawaii. It looked like the moon. He sucked on his water bottle and pushed on.

Dave was now in second place. Mark Allen was in first. He was about five minutes ahead of Dave. Mark had reached the point where the bikes turned around. He and Dave would soon pass each other. It was an important time. Neither of them wanted to look weak. Neither of them wanted to look hurt. So when they passed, both men looked as if they wore masks. They looked as if nothing were wrong.

Suddenly there was a steep downhill. Dave changed gears. Then he changed gears again.

He put his head down and roared down the hill. At the bottom there was a sharp right turn. Scott leaned into the turn. Then he coasted through it with no brakes. When it was done, he thought, "Oooh . . . aaaah. That was risky. I darn near lost it. It was risky all right— and exciting!"

The bike part of a triathlon is the most dangerous. Most of Dave's worst injuries have been from biking. He once skidded on a pile of crushed olives. He hurt his elbow and hip on that one. Another time he hit a dead possum. He flew over his bike and landed on the road. That time he hurt his whole body.

Dave has learned to drink a lot of water. One time years ago, he didn't drink enough water. He pedaled right past an aid station. He thought he could make it to the finish. But his body just dried up. He got dizzy and smashed his bike into a rock. That time he took 60 stitches in his head.

But that was long ago. Now he had to give the Ironman his best. He finished the 112-mile bike ride. While his bike was still rolling, he had his shoes off. Before it had stopped, he had his shirt around his neck. He wasn't going to waste any time. He was still in second place, 11 minutes behind. But he didn't have to be happy about it. Maybe if he dressed fast, he could pick up a few seconds.

It took him about a minute to eat a banana and put on his running shoes. He started to run. It was slow at first. His legs felt like rubber. For 112 miles the bike had held up his weight. Now his legs had to do that work. Dave knew it would get better. He had done this before.

The road was hot. It felt like it might melt his shoes. Dave's feet began to sweat. Soon the only sound he could hear was the squish-squish-squish of his foot inside of his shoe.

He got faster. He looked steady now. He hit

the road hard with his feet. He lacked grace. But he was as strong as a bull. And he could run forever.

After a few miles, he came to one of the 28 aid stations. People stood by the side of the road. They held out cups of water. They also had wet sponges. Dave wanted both.

He moved to the left. He hardly slowed at all. But he reached out and took a cup of water. He drank it all. Then he grabbed another cup. He drank that, too. Then he took a sponge. He dribbled water onto his face. It ran down his neck. It dripped onto his chest and back. "Aaah," he said. It felt so good.

The TV people in their trucks got word to Scott. Mark Allen was now only six minutes ahead. He had leg cramps. He was slowing to a walk. The news gave Scott a jolt. It was like someone had plugged him in. Like a cat after a mouse, he picked up the pace and set off after Allen.

When Scott caught him, Allen was hurting. He was walking under the hot sun. He could not go any faster. Scott ran by him and never looked back. He had Allen right where he wanted him. He would win another Ironman.

———

Dave Scott is a pro triathlete. At first, he raced for love of the sport. Now he races for love and money. Most triathlons have prize money for the winners. He also gets money from sponsors. Those are companies that pay to have their name on Dave's shoes or bike. People see the names on TV. Then they will buy more shoes and bikes. That is the way the companies think.

Dave also makes money as a teacher. Most people do not have any idea how to train for a triathlon. They come to him. He sets up classes to teach them.

Yes, Dave is in it for the money. But he is also in it for love. He loves the sport. It has been good to him. And he has been good for the sport.

But the sport is also a job. Getting up at 6:00 a.m. on a foggy morning is part of that job. Biking 100 miles in the cold is part of the job. Like all workers, Dave sometimes feels like calling in sick. He says, "I'm human. Some days I just feel like sitting in my bean bag chair and letting the day go by."

Elaine Mariolle on the RAAM Trail

Elaine Mariolle
RAAM Rider

Elaine Mariolle is the oldest of 11 kids. Like her brothers and sisters, she always liked sports. But since she stood only 5 feet 2 inches tall as an adult, she was too small for many sports.

She liked being outside, so she tried running. Then in 1983 she bought a bike. "I had no plan of racing across the country. I did not even know there was such a race," she says.

At a cycling picnic one day, she watched a video of the 1983 Race Across America (RAAM). She watched with great interest as the racers fought their way across the country. They looked to Elaine like soldiers in battle.

She recalls, "They were eating and brushing their teeth by the side of the road. It looked like the hardest thing in the world. My plan right then was to do it next year."

A year later at the start of the 1984 RAAM, a nervous Elaine cried in her hotel room. Her goal was to bike from coast to coast in 11 days. But mostly she just wanted to finish. She wanted it so bad, it hurt. She forced down some oatmeal. Then she put on her pink and purple cycling outfit.

A little later she was standing next to her bicycle at the starting line for the RAAM. She squinted east. She had no hope of seeing the finish line. It was 3,047 miles away in Atlantic City. But it was just fun to imagine.

At 9:00 a.m., the mayor of Huntington Beach, California, fired a gun to start the race. There were lots of people there to watch.

The riders rode from the beach onto the city streets. The pace was controlled for the first 45 minutes. They rode at an easy speed of 15-16 miles per hour.

Elaine rode next to veteran cyclist Susan Notorangelo. She asked Susan if it helped having been in the RAAM before. Susan replied, "No. It just reminds you how much it will hurt."

The race really began after the 45 minutes of paced riding. The race director waved a flag. The cyclists took off in a blur of color. Going into the race, Elaine knew she could not win. She was new to the sport. "I just wanted to make it from the West Coast to the East Coast. I had come for the thrill and the adventure. And to learn," she says.

Elaine headed for Las Vegas. It was hot and overcast as she started the 26 mile climb out of the Los Angeles basin. She was in last place. The only people in the race behind her were her crew members. They followed in a car and a mobile home.

She was right where she thought she would be. But it still upset her. "No one likes to be in last place. I was depressed," she says.

It got worse. After dark, a huge rain storm struck. Her rain gear was poor and she was quickly soaked. As a TV announcer said, "You have to expect the weird in a race like RAAM." It would have been easy for Elaine to quit. But she kept going.

Elaine was now in Nevada. Twenty-four hours after the start, Elaine had biked 312 miles without sleep. It was her best distance ever for 24 hours. She was pleased by the mileage. But she was not pleased by how far she was behind the leaders.

She stopped for her first sleep break at the Arizona-Utah border. It was early afternoon. She was 406 miles into the race. Her crew put her to bed in the tiny motor home. It was hot and cramped. Flies kept buzzing in her nose and mouth. She could not sleep. That day she learned an important lesson. She must never try to sleep when the sun was up.

Elaine was 535 miles into the race after two days. Her biggest problem was chafing from riding in the rain. She says, "It hurt so to sit on the saddle. I tried creams and saddle pads. I even changed the way I sat. Nothing seemed to help. But there was no way I was going to drop out because my butt hurt."

It was Utah, with its strange rocks, where she first began to see things. Rocks and bushes began to look like animals. She tried to ignore it. Maybe it would go away. But it got worse. At one point a huge rock turned into a monster cat. The cat snarled and Elaine screamed. She swerved toward the white line. That frightened her crew. They quickly pulled her from the bike and put her to bed.

In Colorado, Elaine and her crew were getting cranky. She says, "Everyone was tired. No one had slept enough. The newness of the first days had worn off. And we still had 2,000 miles to go!"

Part of her liked the crew's care and help. But she missed being alone. And she also felt bad that she was so far behind the leaders. She was more than a day behind by this time. "It had begun to sink in just how long a race the RAAM really was," she says.

Loveland Pass, 12,000 feet above sea level, was the highest point on the course. It was a killer climb for most people. But Elaine liked the mountains. They gave her a mental lift.

She did well climbing Loveland Pass. She passed a line of touring cyclists. It felt great to catch other cyclists even if they weren't in the race. As she neared the top, her crew played the theme song from the movie "Rocky." She felt like a hero.

At the top they stopped for a few minutes and took pictures. They enjoyed the moment. Then it was down the mountain into gathering darkness and rain. She rode through Denver and out into the plains.

Elaine thought she would make good time through the Midwest. After all, Kansas is flat. But it is also windy, as she found out. And the wind was blowing right in her face. It slowed her speed and broke her heart.

She watched a thunder storm build ahead. The sky grew black. "It was so dark. There were clouds and lightning all around. I was being blown all over the road. The veins of lightning were wild and scary. I saw myself as a human lightning rod," she says.

Elaine rode on. The crew fed her meals bite by bite as she pedaled. She was afraid to let go of the handlebars to eat. Finally she had to quit for the night outside some little town in Kansas.

The next day she made a stupid mistake. She said she needed to be alone. Her crew went up ahead. She pulled off and lay down in some tall grass and quickly fell asleep. When the crew could not find her, they got scared. They drove around for an hour looking for her. They were afraid that she had been killed. When they finally found her, everyone yelled and screamed. Then they all felt better.

Elaine had ridden 2,000 miles by the time she reached Missouri. She liked the smell of the trees there. She liked the big bugs and bullfrogs croaking in the night air. But then she got word that the men's leader, Pete Penseyres, was close to the finish line in Atlantic City. She was just outside St. Louis, not even to the Mississippi River. Would she ever get there?

Then, after St. Louis, Elaine went through a change. She felt herself get stronger. Both her mind and body felt great. "After 2,000 miles I felt better than I did when I started," she says.

After 2,500 miles, Elaine crossed the Ohio River and rode into West Virginia. "With all the climbing, riding through West Virginia was hard to do. And I didn't like seeing all the poor people there. But I did like the lush, green Appalachian Mountains," she says.

At Philadelphia Elaine had only 100 miles to go. It hit her then that she had biked 2,900 miles. She was almost there. She would finish!

In Atlantic City, her crew chief got out of the car and ran next to her. He helped her through the busy beach crowd. She recalls that day as if it were last week. She says, "After riding 3,000 miles, I didn't know where I was going. We asked a janitor if this was where the bike race ended. He said, 'What race?' "

Elaine had crossed the finish line in a time of 13 days, 23 hours, 36 minutes. She was the third and last woman to finish. But it seems the race officials went home after 11 days. They said that a cyclist who reached Atlantic City after 11 days was not an "official" finisher. She knew better. She had finished all right. She had the saddle sores to prove it. What's more, she was coming back next year to do it again.

Elaine did come back the next year. She was smarter and in better shape. It showed. She finished three days faster. Her time was 10 days, 23 hours, 40 minutes.

Her time was better, but she was still the third woman to finish. It was not good enough. Even though she hurt a nerve in her hand, she knew she would be back in 1986. She wanted to win!

So she trained even harder. She now rode her bike at least 500 miles every week. One week she rode 1,000 miles! She was as ready as she could be.

In 1986 she raced in the RAAM for the third straight year. Again she got better. This time she was the first woman to cross the finish line with a time of 10 days, 2 hours, 4 minutes. That was the fastest any woman had ever ridden a bike from coast to coast.

Three years after buying her first bike, Elaine was a world record holder. She was asked what winning the Race Across America has been worth to her.

She thought about it. Then she said, "I've become a lot stronger person. It has changed my feelings about life. I think more about each day. I try to make every day worth something. I probably will not be riding a bike all my life. But the things I get out of racing are things I can use when I am 105 years old."

Why did she demand so much of herself?

"I want to know I have been alive. I want to know that I have felt something. Win, lose or tie, I have to try. There is no way I can know what I am made of unless I try. And when my racing days are over, I will know it. And it will be O.K. This is, after all, just one chapter in a whole book of adventures."

John Bachar—Man Against Mountain

John Bachar
Rock Star

On a hot September day in Yosemite, John Bachar puts on his climbing boots. He stares at the high wall of stone in front of him. He shuts his eyes. He sees himself doing a 250-foot climb. It is the one called "Crack-A-Go-Go."

After John sees himself climbing Crack-A-Go-Go in his mind, he will do it. That is why he is different from most others who have come before him. Another thing that makes him different is that he climbs alone. He does not use ropes or pitons. What he does is called free soloing. He is the best in the world at it.

He picks up the gear he will use. It is a bag of chalk to keep his hands dry and snug rock-climbing boots. That is all he needs except for talent, courage, and will power.

He stands and stretches. He is wearing only baggy white shorts and no shirt. He has the strong arms, back, and shoulders needed to be a world-class rock climber. John is listed as 5 feet, 11 inches and 160 pounds. But he looks very small and thin.

Slowly, like a cat, John moves to the rock. He reaches into his bag and dusts his hands. He turns them as white as flour. He places one hand, then the other, on the rock. His finger joints stiffen, growing larger to fill the crack. Then he lifts his right leg as high as his hip. He fits his toe into a hole the size of a postage stamp. He lifts himself off the ground and onto the rock. It takes less strain than most people need to get out of bed.

This is how John starts his climb. In an easy climb he has plenty of time to think. He remembers that his parents did not raise him to climb rocks. They were sure that John would be like his father and teach math. That sounded fine to John. He got straight A's in math through high school. He also played sports. He liked baseball and track. His best event was the pole vault. He remembers, "I dug the pole vault. I tied the school record in practice."

But then he found climbing. By his senior year, he was cutting track practice. He would go to a climbing spot north of Los Angeles called Stony Point. John says, "I started out cutting track just on Wednesdays. The weekend gave me three days to climb. But it was not enough. So I cut Tuesdays and Thursdays, too. By the time I was 16, I could do all the climbing problems at Stony Point. Nobody else could say that."

When it came to climbing, few could keep up with John Bachar. So he learned to climb alone. "I did not have any friends in high school. But I met a few people climbing. Ron Kauk was one," he says.

Ron and John became friends. They were much better climbers than anyone else. They were in a league all their own. When summer ended, Ron wanted John to go with him to live and climb in California's Yosemite National Park. There were endless exciting places to climb in Yosemite. Instead, John went back to Los Angeles. He enrolled in math at the University of California. At the same time Ron moved to Yosemite. There he began climbing new routes. He was becoming well-known.

During his freshman year, John got a C in math. He was thinking of Ron. He was thinking of Yosemite. And he was sad and unhappy. Ron's letters from Yosemite only made it worse. It gave him a desire he had never felt before. Ron wrote, "It is the best climbing in the world! When you do a new route in Yosemite, you get to name it. I have named thirteen already."

John asked his mother what he should do. She knew a thing or two about life. "Do what you love to do," she told him. So the next day he quit the university and went to Yosemite.

John thinks free soloing is the most popular sport in the world. "Everyone free solos. When you walk to the store, you are free soloing. It's just a matter of how hard it is to get there," he says.

In the Yosemite counting system, routes are classed like this:

Class 1: a walk

Class 2: proper shoes needed

Class 3: ropes are advised—not because the course is so hard, but because a fall would mean death

Class 4: everyone—except free soloists—uses ropes

Class 5.0 to 5.14: the important class for most serious climbers. John, however, will not even sniff at a climb less than 5.10.

It makes sense that John is a great rock climber. He loves the sport so much. When he talks about it, he gets as bright-eyed as a child. You get the feeling that hardly anyone has ever loved a thing as much as John loves climbing. He says, "It's great. I cannot understand why people play baseball when they could be climbing. It's so much fun. It is outdoors and beautiful. It also makes you think. It gives you the chance to be afraid, then overcome it. And the sport is so natural. Little boys are always climbing trees, aren't they?"

But what about the danger? What about dying? After all, 300 days a year John is in what he calls "Zone Three." That means if you fall, you die. Most people, like the park rangers, think he is crazy or has a death wish. But it just is not so. John says, "People always talk about the dangers of the solo climb. But they don't know that just about every climbing move can be changed. If it's too hard, I can turn around and go back. You can't do that in speed skiing or hang gliding."

Also, he says that free soloing has another built-in safety feature. "Someone who does not know what he is doing is not going to get very far up a 5.11 climb. The beginner will drop out long before Zone 3." (The numbers tell us that is true. Of the 850 climbing deaths in the United States between 1951 and 1984, only one was from a free-solo rock climbing fall.)

John himself has taken only one bad fall. One day he was climbing in Colorado and dropped 20 feet. His great balance let him land on his feet. A loosened rock then knocked him down, badly bruising his back. He stood up, fainted, came to, and drove himself home. He is a tough guy.

Yes, John is tough but not fearless. He just knows how to control fear. He makes it work for him. "Fear of falling makes me pay attention," he says. "I zoom right in. But it's a relaxed sort of thinking. You hear people say you shouldn't look down. But I look down all the time. It's beautiful up there."

To climb Zone 3, a climber must be very strong. When John is not climbing, he is usually working out in the outdoor gym he built in a Yosemite Valley forest. One of the things he has there is a 2"x8" board nailed between two pine trees. Blocks of wood are nailed to the big board. They give him small holds for one-armed fingertip pull-ups. The Guiness Book of World Records says that only one person out of every 100,000 can do a single one-armed pull-up. But John does many one-armed fingertip pull-ups. And he does them with barbell weights tied to his waist!

He says, "I do more than is necessary. I want to be stronger than I will ever need up on the rock."

A world-class rock climber has to have a

strong mind, too. Like a chess champ, John must think many moves ahead. All the math he studied, he believes, helped train his mind for solving problems on the rock. Sometimes when he is up there, he plays mind games. "I pretend that a light switch in my body was just turned on and that electric power is racing through me," he says. "It works great for a two-second move."

The Yosemite guide books give us a clue as to how special John is. They say that Fairview Dome near Tuolumne Meadows is a 5-8 hour round-trip climb. John has done it bottom to top in 17 minutes. It is 1200 feet and very steep. If that is not enough, he has climbed both El Capitan and Half Dome in the same day.

Even if he slows down, John plans to climb until he dies. It is not that he wants to die, he is quick to point out. He just accepts that it could happen. "No matter what we do with our lives, our bodies are only here for awhile," he adds. "We are all going to die. I would rather die climbing than doing anything else. Better there than in some dumb car crash."

When he puts it that way, he doesn't sound so crazy.